Quackers, the Troublesome Duck

by Leslie Ellen
Illustrated by Leanne Franson

Modern Curriculum Press
Parsippany, New Jersey

Cover and book design by Dorothea Fox

Modern Curriculum Press
An imprint of Pearson Learning
299 Jefferson Road, P.O. Box 480
Parsippany, NJ 07054–0480

www.pearsonlearning.com

1-800-321-3106

ISBN 0-7652-0878-4

7 8 9 10 11 12 13   MA   07 06 05 04 03

CONTENTS

To Toby and Dennis—"Quack!"

Chapter 1
A Duck Named Quackers

A gentle April breeze was blowing as Jody Martin and Ben Stubbs walked through Quincy Park on their way to school. They were walking near the pond as they usually did each weekday morning and afternoon.

Jody's long dark hair blew around her face as she said, "Look at the buds on the trees. I bet it won't be long before they blossom and the flowers bloom."

"Mmmmm, just smell the wonderful smells. I love spring!" said Ben.

Ben, whose sharp blue eyes missed nothing, saw a movement in some tall grass.

"Jody," he said, "wait a minute."

Ben walked over to where he thought he saw something moving.

"Jody," said Ben, "come quick!"

"Is this an April Fool's joke?" Jody asked. She knew how much Ben loved to make jokes.

"No!" shouted Ben. "Look at this!"

"Wow!" was all Jody could say when she saw what Ben found so interesting. "It's an egg, and it's CRACKING!"

"It looks too big to be a chicken egg," said Ben.

Jody, whose favorite subject was science, said, "I'll bet it's a duck egg. Lots of ducks live around the duck pond all spring and summer."

"Let's stay and watch what happens," said Ben.

Jody looked at her watch. "We're going to be very late for school," she replied.

"Oh, come on!" Ben pleaded.

Jody and Ben kneeled in the grass and watched. They couldn't take their eyes off the light blue egg that was wiggling and jiggling in the grass.

After a while, a small duckling worked its way out of the shell. Ben and Jody were the first things the little duckling saw.

They laughed at the funny things the duckling did as its feathers dried in the April sunshine. They watched the duckling as it tumbled and peeped.

"You're even trying to quack already," said Ben, who loved animals—especially baby animals.

"I think we should call the duck Quackers," said Ben with a grin.

The children didn't know that as they were watching the duckling, the duckling was watching them.

"Jody, Quackers is really cute. But now we're late for school. How will we explain this to Ms. Ramos?" Ben asked.

"That's what I told you," said Jody. "Now we really have to hurry."

Jody and Ben rushed out of the park. They practically ran the short distance to Parkside School.

When Jody and Ben got to their classroom, their teacher, Ms. Ramos, said, "Jody, Ben, you two are over one hour late. I think you'd better go downstairs and report to Mr. Clark in the principal's office."

"I guess we're in trouble now," said Ben.

"It was worth it!" Jody said.

Jody and Ben did as Ms. Ramos asked. Just as they were leaving the principal's office, they saw an amazing sight. In the doorway of the school was a little duckling.

"Quackers!" shouted Jody and Ben together.

"It looks like the duck followed us to school! What will we do now?" asked Ben.

Chapter 2
Duck+Pizza=Trouble

Everyone in the class wanted to keep Quackers. Ms. Ramos thought about it, then decided that Quackers could stay for a while. Almost two months passed. The class raised the duck and watched it grow. From a fuzzy brown and yellow duckling, it quickly became an active adult female mallard. It had tan, brown, and white feathers and orange legs and feet.

There were some people who thought Quackers was too active. Time after time, Quackers seemed to get into trouble.

On a warm day in June, Ms. Ramos's class was doing a math lesson. Ben, who loved math, was trying hard to pay attention to Ms. Ramos. Ms. Ramos was drawing circles on the chalkboard. Each circle stood for a pizza. Each pizza circle was divided into a different number of pieces. One showed halves. One showed fourths. One showed eighths—the same number of pieces as a REAL pizza.

As a treat, Ms. Ramos got pizza for the class to have for lunch. Four pizza boxes were waiting on a table at the back of the room.

"Jody," whispered her friend Tina Perez, "what is Quackers up to now?"

Jody turned around and saw Quackers standing with her two big orange feet right in the middle of one of the pizzas. She had gotten one of the pizza boxes open. Quackers was having a wonderful time. She was eating pizza.

"Oh no!" cried Jody. "Quackers is in trouble again!"

Ms. Ramos, who had been facing the chalkboard, quickly turned around. She was just in time to see Quackers jump out of the pizza box.

Quackers had a long string of cheese hanging from her bill. As she waddled across the table and onto the floor, she left a webbed-footed trail of tomato sauce footprints.

"The time has come for Quackers to GO!" said Ms. Ramos.

Chapter 3
Goodbye, Quackers

Quackers walked over to Ben, whom she followed everywhere. Ben quickly grabbed some paper towels and cleaned the duck's feet. Jody and Tina wiped the floor and the table.

Ms. Ramos gave the children pizza from the boxes that Quackers hadn't touched.

Ms. Ramos said, "I'm afraid the time has come to return Quackers to the place where Ben and Jody found her. She will be happier living near the duck pond with other ducks like herself."

"Nooooooo!" cried the class. "What will we do without Quackers?"

Ms. Ramos had made up her mind. Ben and Jody led the line of students as the whole class left the school building. Ben was holding Quackers.

The duck seemed happy to be in Ben's arms. It wasn't long before they left the city sidewalk and entered the path that led to Quincy Park Duck Pond. "Do we have to let Quackers go?" moaned Ben.

"I'm afraid so," said Ms. Ramos.

Together, Ben and Jody put Quackers in the water. Quackers began to swim. She put her head in the water and began to look for food. Ms. Ramos looked at Jody and Ben's sad faces and smiled kindly.

"Quackers really will be better off here. You'll see," she said.

The class walked slowly out of the park
on their way back to school. They were just
in time to see Quackers stick her whole
head and neck into the water. Nothing but
tail feathers showed.

Just as the children walked out of sight,
Quackers began to follow them.

Chapter 4

Quackers Goes to Kindergarten

When they got back to the classroom, everyone took a seat. They settled down to work on a social studies project. The students were making a model of their neighborhood out of cereal boxes, cardboard, and clay.

Suddenly, everyone heard a loud QUACK.

Ben and his friend Brad Ming quickly looked up from the clay people they were making.

"Look, Ben," said Brad, "it's Quackers!"

"QUACKERS!" shouted Ben.

Ben put down the clay he was holding and ran over to Quackers. He lifted the duck off her feet and took her to Ms. Ramos.

"Ms. Ramos, Quackers is back!"

"Not again," sighed Ms. Ramos. "I'm afraid you and Jody will have to take Quackers right back to the pond, Ben. Quackers is just too big to keep in our classroom," Ms. Ramos explained. "I'm sure Mr. Clark will be happy to walk you two and Quackers back to the park."

Jody went over to Ben who was still holding Quackers.

"Let's go," she said.

Once again, Jody and Ben carried Quackers out of Parkside School. Along with Mr. Clark, they walked Quackers back to the pond in Quincy Park.

Soon after Jody and Ben returned, work in Ms. Ramos's classroom stopped again. This time they heard the sound of children's screams and laughter. It was coming from the classroom below.

"What's happening downstairs in Mr. Fleet's kindergarten class?" Ms. Ramos wondered. "The afternoon kindergarten is usually so quiet we don't even know they are there."

It wasn't long before they heard the sound of quacking coming from the floor below. Jody and Ben gave each other a look and raced out of the classroom. Ms. Ramos and the others were close behind.

When they got downstairs, they saw kindergarten children running in all directions. Chairs were turned over. Crayons and paints were everywhere. Mr. Fleet didn't know which child to help first.

In the middle of everything was Quackers. She chased one child and then another. She was having a wonderful time. To Quackers this was the best kind of game.

All of a sudden, Quackers saw the
children's water table. Small boats, cups,
and little dolls went sailing overboard as
Quackers flew into the water. Calmly,
Quackers began to smooth her feathers.

At that moment Mr. Clark rushed in.

"WHAT'S GOING ON NOW?" he asked.

Chapter 5

Trouble in the Cafeteria

"I don't understand," said Mr. Clark, "I thought we returned Quackers to the duck pond in Quincy Park."

"We did, but it seems Quackers keeps coming back!" replied Ms. Ramos.

"Well, we've got to try again," said Mr. Clark. "Quackers is getting into too much trouble. She must go back to her home at the pond."

Mr. Clark began to help Mr. Fleet bring peace to the kindergarten. Ms. Ramos and the class carried Quackers back to their room.

"It's almost time to go home," said Ms. Ramos. "We'll let Quackers spend the night."

All the children shouted with joy. "Quackers can stay! Quackers can stay!" they cried.

"TOMORROW," continued Ms. Ramos in a loud, strong voice, "Jody, Ben, and Mr. Clark will try again to take her back to the park. Maybe this time she'll stay put."

The next day Ben and Jody didn't even sit down in their seats when they got to Ms. Ramos's room. They said hello to Ms. Ramos and their friends. Then they walked over to Quackers's pen. They picked her up and carried her out the door. They stopped off at the office so Mr. Clark could join them.

Brad, Tina, and the rest of their friends watched from the second floor window as Ben, Jody, and Mr. Clark took the duck back to Quincy Park Duck Pond again.

"We're back," Ben called out as he and Jody returned to their classroom.

They joined their classmates, who had just begun to watch a video about birds.

"When the birds hatch, they follow their mothers everywhere," said the narrator of the video. "This is called *imprinting*. Sometimes another kind of animal is the first thing a baby bird sees.

When this happens, the bird thinks that this animal is its mother.

"Birds have even been known to imprint on people. Sometimes this happens when all of the other birds in a nest have hatched. The mother has wandered away with them and the last one is left alone. The little orphan will imprint on the first creature it sees."

"THAT'S IT!" shouted Ben. "Quackers must have imprinted on Jody and me!"

"I agree with Ben," said Jody slowly as though she were figuring out the answer to a science experiment. "That must be why she keeps coming back!"

"You may be right," said Ms. Ramos as she turned off the video. "But don't worry. Quackers is old enough now to get along on her own."

All at once, everyone heard the sound of many plastic cafeteria trays hitting the floor. Children were laughing. Grown-ups were yelling.

"It sounds like the noise is coming from the cafeteria," said Ms. Ramos.

Once again the class rushed out of the room to see what was going on.

When they got to the cafeteria, everyone knew that Quackers had come back again. A tall stack of trays had been knocked over. Plates, knives, forks, and spoons were all over the floor.

Children were laughing. Grown-ups were screaming. In the middle of it all, there was Quackers. Her orange feet were covered in mounds of mashed potatoes. Potatoes were dripping from her head and her bill.

When Quackers saw Ben and Jody, she
let out a loud, happy, "QUACK!" From way
down the hall they could hear the sound of
Mr. Clark's voice saying, "NOW WHAT'S
GOING ON?"

Chapter 6

Far, Far Away

"I had a funny feeling that I would find you and your class here, Ms. Ramos," said Mr. Clark. "I see our feathered friend is back again."

"We just saw a video about mallards, Mr. Clark," said Ben in a rush. "We learned that ducks can imprint on people. Quackers must have imprinted on Jody and me."

"Then I think I have to take matters into my own hands," said Mr. Clark. "I am going to call the city's Save Our Wildlife Association. In the meantime, Quackers is coming with me."

Mr. Clark lifted Quackers and held her out in front of him. He carried Quackers out of the cafeteria.

Ms. Ramos, Ben, Jody, and the class followed close behind.

Mr. Clark went up the stairs to the second floor. Across the hall from Ms. Ramos's classroom was a closed door. A sign on the door said Storage.

Mr. Clark opened the door. Ben and Jody peeked in. They could see boxes filled with papers. Many, many old books were on the shelves.

"I think Quackers will be safe in here until someone from the Save Our Wildlife Association gets here," said Mr. Clark. He put Quackers down and closed the door.

"Everyone back to your classroom," said Mr. Clark.

Quackers was left alone.

Chapter 7
FIRE!

Jody, Ben, and the rest of the class walked sadly back to their classroom.

"Quackers can't stay in that messy little room all alone," said Jody worriedly.

"She'll be fine," said Ms. Ramos. "It will only be for a little while. Someone from the Save Our Wildlife Association will be here soon."

Ms. Ramos had just begun reading to the class when they heard loud quacks coming from the storage room.

"That's Quackers," said Jody. "I bet she's in trouble."

"I'm sure she's all right," said Ms. Ramos. "She is probably just unhappy about being alone."

Ms. Ramos went back to reading. The quacking went on and on. In fact, it seemed to get louder and louder. Ben and Jody gave each other troubled looks.

The quacking continued.

"Maybe Quackers is hurt," wondered Tina.

"Or maybe she just doesn't like to be in such a small space," added Brad.

"Ms. Ramos," shouted Ben suddenly. "I can't stand it anymore. I'm going to see if Quackers is all right!"

"I'm coming, too," said Jody.

Ben and Jody rushed out of the room with Tina, Brad, Ms. Ramos, and the rest of the class close behind. Ben flung open the door of the storage room. Out came a cloud of smoke. Out flew Quackers.

"Oh my goodness!" shouted Jody.
"There's a fire!"

Chapter 8

Our Hero

Ms. Ramos pulled the fire alarm on the wall. Then she sprayed the flames. The fire bell began to ring. Ben picked up Quackers and everyone filed out of the building.

Everyone in Parkside School was out on the sidewalk. In a very short time, two big fire trucks arrived. Firefighters went into the building. Soon, the fire chief came out to speak to Mr. Clark.

"The fire seems to have started in a storage room on the second floor," said the fire chief.

"Yes, well, we were storing a duck in that storage room," began Mr. Clark.

"A DUCK?" asked the fire chief.

"Yes," said Jody, "a duck. You see, my friend, Ben, and I found this duck egg. It was all alone. When it hatched, the duck imprinted on us. That means that the duck thought that Ben and I were its parents."

"We TRIED to return the duck to the pond in the park where we found her," Ben said. "But Quackers kept coming back. Then Mr. Clark put Quackers in the storage room. Quackers didn't mean to start a fire," wailed Ben.

"Slow down, slow down," said the fire chief. "The fire was caused by old wiring. The room must not have been used very much. There were boxes and papers too close to the plug."

"The duck was in the storage room because she kept getting into trouble," said Ms. Ramos. "When we heard all the quacking, we went to check on Quackers. That's when we found the fire."

"It seems to me that you have a real hero on your hands," the fire chief said to Mr. Clark. "If it hadn't been for the duck's quacking, the fire might have spread."

"Quackers is a hero! We HAVE to keep Quackers now," said Ben.

"Just a minute," said Mr. Clark. "I agree. Quackers is a wonderful duck. She saved our school. But we cannot keep a full-grown mallard at Parkside School."

At that moment, everyone heard a quacking sound. It wasn't Quackers.

"Look," said Jody, "up in the sky."

Overhead they saw a flock of mallards. Ben put Quackers down.

Quackers looked up. She saw the ducks. She began to run. Then Quackers stopped. She looked back at Ben and Jody. Finally, Quackers spread her wings and took off into the sky.

"Quackers, come back!" cried Ben.
"Quackers, stop! Come back!" called
Jody as she began to run after the duck.
It was no use. Quackers was flying away.

Chapter 9

Gone But Not Forgotten

Everyone was quiet. They stood in amazement looking up at the sky. The flock of ducks was almost out of sight.

No one heard the white van pull up at the curb. It stopped right behind the fire trucks. A young woman got out and walked over to Mr. Clark.

"Are you Mr. Clark?" she asked. "I'm Carol Chase from the Save Our Wildlife Association."

Mr. Clark looked bewildered. He said, "It seems our mallard just flew away."

Ms. Chase shaded her eyes and looked up at the sky. "There they go," she said.

"Things in Ms. Ramos's class sure will be different without Quackers," said Jody thoughtfully. "Quackers was a real hero," she added.

"Quackers saved our school from a fire," said Ben softly. "Now she's gone."

Mr. Clark and Ms. Ramos told Carol Chase all about how Ben and Jody found Quackers. They told her about how the class raised Quackers and all of the things they learned about ducks. Mr. Clark told Carol Chase about all of the trouble Quackers had gotten into lately, but now he had a small smile on his face.

"Here is a poster of a family of mallards. It will remind you of Quackers," she said.

She added, "Don't worry. I don't think you've lost Quackers. Your hero will probably come back next spring. Mallards usually come back to their nesting grounds. Quackers probably will be starting a family of her own."

"Oh boy," said Ben, "I can hardly wait!"

Jody said, "We can raise more ducklings next spring!"

Mr. Clark and Ms. Ramos gave each other a worried look. Then they looked at Ben and Jody.

Jody and Ben were looking up at the sky. They watched as the flock of ducks disappeared out of sight. Then they looked at each other and smiled.

GLOSSARY

cafeteria (kaf uh TIHR ee uh) a place to eat where people are served at a counter and carry their own food to a table

female (FEE mayl) a woman, a girl, or any animal of this sex

hero (HEE roh) a person who has become very important and honored, usually for performing brave deeds

imprinting (ihm PRIHNT ihng) fixing firmly in memory, such as a baby bird becomes strongly attached to the first moving thing it sees

mallard (MAL urd) a kind of wild duck that lives in the United States and Canada

orphan (OR fun) a person or animal without a mother and father

storage room (STOR ihj room) a room where things are put away for later use

troublesome (TRUB ul sum) disturbing; giving trouble

video (VIHD ee oh) a film in a plastic case that can be put into a television to show a program

waddled (WAHD uld) walked with short swaying steps